Choose A Career

And

Discover Your

Perfect Job

105 Tips On
Work Attitude
And Motivation

By Gary Vurnum & Patrick Merlevede

www.jobEQ.com

Choose A Career And Discover Your Perfect Job: 105 Tips On Work Attitude And Motivation

ISBN: 1456302795
EAN-13: 9781456302795

For author contact information, go to: **www.merlevede.biz**

Introduction

We all have our own strengths and weaknesses. This is reflected in your attitude and what motivates you - as we all pay more attention to the things we like and we try to 'ignore' the things we don't!

It therefore makes sense to focus on your strengths and to attempt to organize your job in such a way so that it is compatible with what you like doing and what you are good at.

However, you may not really understand what your strengths are, and we all have 'blind spots' which, often unconsciously, hold us back from truly making the most of our lives.

With this is mind, jobEQ has identified 48 'patterns' linked to these strengths and weaknesses or likes and dislikes, each of which you should not only be aware of, but make an effort to address where applicable.

In this book you will find two simple and immediately actionable tips for each of these patterns.

Although you can read them as you would a normal book, it is also useful to take one tip each day and work with it to see how you can implement it into your life. Don't let the simplicity of these tips fool you. Just apply them in your life and you'll see how powerful they really are!

When you take the time to focus on one tip each day, these 105 Tips are an agenda for the next 15 weeks.

Combining this book with the iWAM questionnaire will allow you to discover your own key strengths and development areas; you can try out the iWAM for free at **www.jobEQ.net/SelfTest**

How To Use This Book For Choosing A Career Or Discovering Your Perfect Job

Study after study linked to money and happiness show that when we have to choose between two jobs, of which one pays more but seems less interesting and the other one is paid less but seems much more fun, people tend to choose the job that is paid the best.

However, what happy people know is that when choosing for a job, you should go for the job that you think you will like the most. The trap is that we think that money will make us happy, while in reality our happiness comes from the activities that we do.

Moreover, when you have more fun doing the things you need to do, you are likely to be better at it as well...and even become better at it as experience grows. As an effect, people tend to develop the skills which they like and become even better at them.

While the tips in this book can be used to help you to discover areas where you might need to develop yourself, you can also use them as a way to learn more about the areas you like the most. Here is how:

Go over the first ninety-six tips, and indicate for each one whether they already come as naturally or whether they present a challenge for you. Based on that, choose the five patterns which are your key strengths and the five patterns which present your biggest challenge.

The ideal job is the one that corresponds to your strengths, in the sense that your strengths are crucial for the job and that the areas which are challenging for you are not important for the job. If the ones that present your biggest challenge are crucial for your job, it's possible that you have a problem, in the sense that your job might be a stretch, or that your preferences steer you in the direction of self-sabotage: that you tend to "forget" issues which are seen as more important by others...

An example: If you don't like to work with people, a job in sales or customer care may be a challenge if one of the requirements of the job is that you develop a close tie with the customer. On the other hand, jobs like bookkeeping or computer programming won't require as much people skills.

When applying for a job, even if the person at the other side of the table would not be asking the question, offer to tell them what your biggest strengths are, as well as the areas you consider challenging. Ask questions to determine to what extent your strengths will be an asset on that job. Maybe you will discover that some of your strengths aren't "appreciated" in that organization. Acting upon them in that context is like shooting yourself in the foot. Also ask questions to determine for yourself whether the challenging factors won't hold you back in that job. Missing these skills may be like falling over the same stone time after time…

Initiative

Trust your judgment to make the right decisions and just go for it!

1

Learn to trust your gut feelings and take more chances than you are usually comfortable with. Successful people take chances then work with their results, as they know that just making a start is the hardest part of the process!

Initiative

Take action first - then analyze.

2

You are the ONLY person responsible for whether you succeed or fail, so you must not allow yourself to get tied down by believing that you need to know everything before you start. Just get going and you'll soon see that taking one step at a time is more productive than planning!

Reflection and Patience

Be patient when things don't go according to plan.

3

Be careful to not let your emotions dictate what you need to do when problems crop up. Make an effort to detach yourself, take a deep breath, and carefully analyze what needs to be done, and only then, make a decision about how best to deal with the issue!

Reflection and Patience

Make quick decisions - but never rush them.

4

It doesn't take long to understand what needs to be done once you have all the information you need to make an informed decision. You never purposely make 'bad' decisions - just ones that end up appearing that way because you weren't fully aware of all the options available at the time!

Goal Orientation

Unless you know what you really want, you'll never achieve it.

5

You wouldn't get on a plane without knowing its destination, so why wouldn't you want to have a destination in life to aim for? You need goals as otherwise you will just wake up in five years time and realize that you are no better off than you are now! Is that what you really want?

Goal Orientation

Have something to measure your progress against, no matter how small.

6

You will never know whether you are moving forward in life unless you have something to measure yourself against. You'll be surprised at how easy it is to achieve your goals when you are consistently checking whether you are moving towards them or not!

Problem Solving

Look at problems as a positive challenge.

7

Every problem has the seed of its solution within it if you look hard enough. No 'failure' is permanent - it is just a temporary defeat which, if you learn from it, will provide you with more insight than if it never happened in the first place!

Problem Solving

Fail falling forward.

8

It is believed that Thomas Edison made 10,000 attempts at making a light bulb before discovering the method that worked. He did so because he knew that what he was trying to achieve was possible...he just had to keep 'failing' until, by a process of elimination, he would arrive at the solution.

Individual Motives

Believe in yourself.

9

You're capable of achieving so much more in life than you could ever possibly imagine, so don't be your own worst enemy by fooling yourself that you're not good enough. Make your own decisions based on what YOU want, and don't let other people make them for you!

Individual Motives

Have confidence in your decisions.

10

Have faith in your own ability, and don't wait for approval or validation from others before making decisions - especially where the direction of your life is concerned! You're the only person who will have to deal with the results of your decisions - so start making them for yourself!

External Reference

Learn to accept constructive criticism.

11

Sometimes, we can get so close to something that we lose sight of the bigger picture, so allow yourself to accept feedback from others without taking it personally. You should always welcome another opinion as it will give you the opportunity of a different perspective.

External Reference

Make the most of other peoples' knowledge.

12

Everyone is weak and strong in different areas. So, don't ignore other people around you whom have relevant experience, as they will help you succeed more quickly than by doing everything yourself. It's not a sign of weakness to ask other people for help as successful people do it all the time!

Alternatives (Options)

There is ALWAYS another way!

13

It is often the case that your first attempt will fail. Don't be like most people and give up at the first attempt, as there will always be different ways to achieve what you need to if you look hard enough.

Alternatives (Options)

Just because something has always been done a certain way doesn't mean that it is right!

14

The biggest breakthroughs always come from those people who challenge conventional thinking rather than just sticking to what everyone else tells them is 'possible'. Don't hold back if you feel that you want to try something different.

Follow Procedures

Be creative, but don't ignore what already works in the process!

15

An airline pilot needs to stick rigidly to procedures, yet also needs to be willing to deviate from them if an emergency arises. Be like that pilot, and use what already works as a foundation for improvement rather than trying to reinvent the wheel every single time!

Follow Procedures

Even though there may be more exciting things to work on, don't ignore what needs to be done.

16

Make sure that you don't let the 'boring but important' tasks slip when more interesting and challenging tasks come along. Always get the essential things out of the way first before you start working on how to improve them!

Breadth

Don't get so tied up with the details that you miss the bigger picture.

17

No matter what is going on, you always need to keep one eye on the overall objective you are trying to aim for.

Breadth

Don't let perfectionism get in the way of making progress.

18

Of course, there should be a need to do things right, but often 'good enough' is more than acceptable. Aim for a balance between doing things exactly right, and doing it well enough so that you can move forward. Don't let your perfectionism be the cause of procrastination!

Depth Orientation

Always break your goals into manageable tasks.

19

Sometimes, a goal can seem so big and so far away that it's difficult to stay motivated to stay on course. So, make sure that you break down the elements of what you need to do into tasks small enough to complete in only a few days or weeks. This way you will have something to regularly measure your progress against.

Depth Orientation

The first step is all you need to make a start!

20

Yes, it feels better when you have everything lined up in front of you, but don't hold back from making a start if you don't. Just begin with step number one, and you'll be surprised at how easily step number two will appear once you get going!

Affective

There is more to communication than what people say.

21

By all means, listen to what people say, but pay very close attention to how they say it, too! It's often the case that someone will say one thing, but their body language or verbal cues will be hinting at the opposite. Therefore it's very important that you are aware of this as it could save a lot of problems in the long run.

Affective

How you feel about what you do is important too!

22

Many people make the mistake of setting goals that they believe they should aim for, rather than doing so based on what inspires them. Don't get caught up in other peoples' expectations of you, and make sure you aspire towards what really feels right for YOU!

Neutral

Be very clear and precise when you express your opinions.

23

Nobody has had the same life experience, and therefore points of reference, as you. It's important that you are very explicit when you are trying to get your point across. Never assume that others will 'get' what you are talking about, and make sure that you always explain yourself in a way that they can fully understand you!

Neutral

Don't let your emotions get in the way of you understanding the facts of a situation.

24

It's all too easy to let your emotions cloud your judgment. You wouldn't be human if you didn't! However, no matter how strongly you may feel about something, never ignore the true facts in front of you because of it!

Group Environment

Don't allow yourself to get too distracted by others.

25

Other people will always have their opinion but ultimately you are the one who has to live with your decisions and actions! So, by all means take different options on board, but always make the decisions that are in your own best interests.

Group Environment

Make the most of other peoples' talents.

26

The most successful people in the world understand the power of tapping into other peoples' knowledge and skills. It may certainly be possible to do everything on your own, but it will certainly be easier and you'll have more chance of success, if you work closely with other people.

Individual Environment

Become your own manager.

27

There is only one person who can truly motivate you - and that is YOU! Even if you function better with others or as part of a team, ultimately you need to have the discipline to be able to get things done when you're on your own, as there will always be times when you will have to.

Individual Environment

Be in control of your own environment.

28

Very few people give some thought to the space that they live and work in. Is it cluttered or organized? Does it help you concentrate or is it easy to get distracted? A little effort in regards to getting your environment right always pays dividends in the end.

Sole Responsibility

You are the only person responsible for YOUR success!

29

No matter what your situation may be, in the end, YOU alone must stand by your successes and failures. You must not rely on other people to carry you. If you want to be successful then you must stand on your own two feet and go out and get it for yourself!

Sole Responsibility

Be willing to step up and take charge if necessary.

30

It's easy to step back when situations arise that challenge you. However, you'll be surprised at how much you can handle when you really tackle things head-on. Not only that, you'll be recognized as someone whom is ready to take on more responsibility.

Shared Responsibility

Don't ignore the power of working in a team.

31

Even though sometimes it may seem easier to do everything yourself, it is a lot more productive to tap into the collective power of teamwork. At the very least you will achieve a lot more...but I can guarantee that there will be people who would love to do the elements of tasks that you hate!

Shared Responsibility

Allow other people to share in your success.

32

It's not always easy to delegate when you are very close to a project, or if you've been working on it for a while. However, you'll be surprised at how much weight can be lifted off of your shoulders by delegating responsibility for certain tasks to other competent people.

Sameness

You don't always need to change something just because you can.

33

Don't get too attached to the idea that you have to change everything in order to be successful. Sometimes the best thing you can do is work with what you've already got rather than start from scratch. The quote "If it ain't broke, don't try to fix it" is often true for a very good reason!

Sameness

Mix up the routine to make it more interesting and challenging.

34

We all have certain routine tasks that need to be done. It's especially easy to let them slide when more exciting things to do come along. So, in order to make sure you get done what needs to get done, just mix things up a little, and maybe do them in a different way, or a different order.

Evolution

Constantly be looking at how to make improvements.

35

Everything you do can be improved or achieved more effectively if you look hard enough. Most people just accept that things are the way they are and that they cannot be changed. Don't be one of them!

Evolution

Always set goals that push you that help you progress steadily.

36

The easiest way to achieve the big goals in life is to set yourself smaller, more achievable, targets regularly along the way. Not only will you get a sense of accomplishment as you complete them, but you will also find that your big goals won't seem so unattainable after all!

Difference

There is always room for innovation.

37

Most of the things you and I take for granted were once a huge leap of faith in the eyes of their inventor. Always allow yourself some space for some radical thinking, as often such a solution may be a lot more achievable than you might think.

Difference

Change happens - get used to it!

38

Whether you like it or not, change WILL happen! Even if you don't actively look for it, it will catch up with you eventually, so you might as well embrace it instead of fighting it.

Use

There is no excuse for procrastination!

39

The best cure for procrastination is to just start anything, even if it's not the most urgent thing that needs doing. All your mind needs is something to begin work on and, once you get moving, you'll find it a lot easier to start tackling what you have been putting off.

Use

The best way to learn to do something is to do it.

40

Don't worry that you may not have everything you need to see yourself through to the completion of something. The best way is to 'learn on the job', as the feedback you will get from taking action will always be more invaluable than learning about the theory!

Concept

You'll never run out of ideas if you continually look for them.

41

Success comes down as much to developing ideas as it does about implementing them. It's also so much easier to make progress when you have an overall idea or concept of what you are trying to achieve. The solution is always out there if you throw enough ideas at it!

Concept

Be aware of what you're aiming for and why you want to get there.

42

Even though it is important to take action, always make sure that it is actually relevant to what you're trying to achieve. Action for action's sake is almost as bad as no action at all as it won't get you any closer to your goal!

Structure

Get organized!

43

It's easy to waste lots of time chasing information when you don't have it all in one place, or easily to hand. Make sure that, even if it doesn't come naturally, you get yourself organized before you start something. Timing is often critical, so don't run of the risk of wasting it by not being prepared!

Structure

Get what needs to be done down on paper.

44

Written plans and daily task lists are excellent tools for a very good reason! When you use them effectively, they enable you to know exactly what you should be doing whatever distractions may try and get in the way.

Past

Don't ignore your own experience when faced with something new.

45

It's easy to forget that even if your experience isn't exactly relevant to what you are currently doing, the lessons you would have learned from it may well be! Don't leave your past at the door as it may help you in more ways than you think.

Past

You'll always get the same result unless you do something differently!

46

One of the main reasons that people fail consistently, time after time, is that they continue to do almost the same things expecting a different result. Mix things up a little and try things you wouldn't normally do, and you might be surprised at what happens!

Present

Don't let your failures from the past or worries about the future influence how you feel right now.

47

All we really do is live in the now - this very moment. Make sure that, whenever possible, you try to focus ONLY on the task at hand and not let the past or future have an impact upon what you can really achieve NOW.

Present

What can you do NOW - this very minute - to move yourself forward?

48

Momentum is critical in getting things done. Therefore, make sure that you don't put off something that can be done right now, as you never know what might need your attention around the corner.

Future

Dream big - but make sure that it inspires you NOW!

49

Of course you should aim high, but if it doesn't inspire you to take action now, this very minute, then perhaps you should first set a smaller, more achievable, target that does!

Future

Take a step in the right direction every single day.

50

No matter how exciting the future you are aiming for is, unless you take practical steps towards it every day, you will struggle to get there. You may be surprised to discover that all 'overnight successes' have put the necessary hours in order to get themselves into the position to be one!

Power

Power isn't a bad thing if you use it wisely.

51

Power gets a bad press as it's often used by one person, or a group or people, at the expense of others. However, if you use any power you have wisely for a positive benefit - not only for yourself, but for others too - then you'll often be surprised at how much leverage it can give you.

Power

Always make an allowance for 'office politics' but still be your own person.

52

It's much harder to swim against the tide than it is to just go with it - so don't make things more difficult for yourself by ignoring office politics. By all means make your own decisions, but always make sure that you don't ignore the majority view in the meantime.

Affiliation (Popularity)

You can still be liked and get to the top!

53

It's a fallacy that you have to upset people in order to get to the top. Of course, you need to be tough and stand by your own decisions, but you don't have to sacrifice your true personality or integrity along the way in order to do so.

Affiliation (Popularity)

By all means be popular, but only for the right reasons!

54

Of course, it makes sense to be well-liked, but being the office joker, for example, won't earn you respect from the people who matter. Be your own person, but make sure that you are remembered for being a positive and constructive influence.

Achievement (Performance)

Regularly push your comfort zone.

55

You will never make any real progress in your life or your career unless you take chances on things that challenge you. The saying 'feel the fear and do it anyway' is very valuable advice as you will be surprised at how the things you fear the most are never quite as bad as they may seem once you have tackled them.

Achievement (Performance)

The secret of success lies in showing up.

56

Never underestimate what you are truly capable of achieving if you put your mind to it. In organizations people are often admired for the results they achieve. Don't wait for others to do things that you react to – be proactive and take the initiative on your own, and you will be surprised at what you can achieve!

Assertive

Never be afraid to stand your ground if you think you are right.

57

Ultimately, the buck stops with you, so you'd better make sure that if you truly believe in something that you stick with it. By all means, take other peoples' views on board, but don't let them take precedence!

Assertive

There is a fine line between being confident and appearing too assertive.

58

Of course, you should always believe in your own ability – but be very careful about how you show this to others as it is easy to come across as too over-confident. Many people look upon confident people as a threat (as they wish they felt that way but don't) so tread carefully with such people when you are dealing with them.

Indifference

Allow yourself to step outside the lines occasionally.

59

By all means make sure that you get done what needs to get done, but it's also OK to let yourself take a few risks now and again. If you do, you'll discover that life can be so much more exciting and ultimately rewarding.

Indifference

It's OK to feel unmotivated sometimes!

60

Even the most happy and successful people have times where they struggle to stay motivated, or to keep up a certain pace. If this happens to you don't beat yourself up about it - just take a break and give yourself a little breathing space. You'll find that you feel more refreshed and raring to go again once you've done so.

Compliance

Don't fight against rules - use them to your advantage instead.

61

Some people take pleasure in breaking rules just to prove a point, or to show that they can. However, needlessly doing so can be counterproductive as most rules are there for very good reasons that you might not even be aware of!

Compliance

Focus your energy in the right direction.

62

Some people take great pride in fighting against the norm or against the 'establishment'. While this may work in some cases, usually it's just a waste of time and energy which could be better spent making the most of what you already have to work with. Rules don't need to be broken in order for you to succeed!

Tolerance

People will always have different opinions to yours - get used to it!

63

You know yourself from when other people try to impose their opinions on you that you don't like it...so don't do it to others!

Tolerance

The more you allow other people to be themselves, the more it helps you both.

64

When someone feels empowered and responsible for their own success they will automatically work more efficiently. With this in mind, don't try to get other people to fit in with you - just let them do things their own way.

Convinced By Seeing

Picture what your future looks like.

65

Close your eyes and get a picture in your mind of what your ideal life looks like. Who is there, what do you have, where are you, what does it feel like to know you have what you've always wanted? Visualize this as often as you can and you'll find it a lot easier to be inspired to make it all happen!

Convinced By Seeing

Have visual cues to remind you what you're aiming for.

66

It is true that a picture is worth a thousand words - so put some inspiring pictures where you can regularly see them. At the very least - have something inspirational as your screensaver as a constant reminder of what you're trying to achieve.

Convinced By Hearing

Make sure that you actively listen to others.

67

Very few people truly listen to the other person when they are talking as they are too busy thinking about what they themselves are going to say next! So, make an effort to focus your thoughts on what the other person is saying and make sure that you show them that they are being listened to!

Convinced By Hearing

Make the most of other peoples' experience.

68

Nobody goes through life without facing some challenges or without having some experiences to learn from. So, don't ignore the experiences of others as they may be able to easily shorten your learning curve if you ask them.

Convinced By Reading

Aim for a big library - not a big TV!

69

Be a reader, not a watcher! Every person who has ever achieved anything in life is a constant learner. You don't have to be 'widely read' - just focus your attention on learning everything you can about what you are aiming for.

Convinced By Reading

Always make the most of the available research.

70

There is more information on any topic available at your fingertips completely free, so there are no excuses for ignoring the vast research that is out there. Don't stick your head in the sand and assume you know it all - because I can certainly guarantee that you don't!

Convinced By Doing

You never really know or understand until you try.

71

You can never possibly understand where other people are coming from unless you experience things for yourself. Don't be afraid to jump in and try something as you'll always get a better understanding from doing than just learning!

Convinced By Doing

Listen to your feelings before you make a decision.

72

Your feelings about something are an excellent guide to whether a certain decision is right for you or not. Most people spend more time worrying about hurting other peoples' feelings rather than how they could be compromising their own! If you constantly make decisions at your own expense you will never be happy.

Convinced By Examples

Never underestimate the power of using examples to prove your point.

73

People have their own opinions for very good reasons so it's not easy to convince them to understand your point of view. Therefore, it will be much easier to get them to more easily appreciate where you are coming from if you give them as many 'real life' examples as possible.

Convinced By Examples

Don't ignore the evidence if it's in front of you!

74

Don't be so stubborn to assume that you are always right, even if the evidence in front of you says otherwise. It is one thing to play devil's advocate, but it's another to purposely go against something that plainly already works!

Convinced Automatically

Always give others the benefit of the doubt.

75

Of course, you should always trust your own judgment - but also allow yourself to trust the judgment of others, too! People don't consciously make bad decisions, so give someone the benefit of the doubt if things don't quite go according to plan.

Convinced Automatically

Stick with your first choice as it's usually the right one.

76

Most of us make a quick decision, and then gradually allow that voice inside our head to talk us out of it! Sure, it your first choice may not always end up being the right one, but you'll have more chance of success if you stick with it rather than talking yourself out of it!

Convinced By Consistency

Never give up on something if it's important to you.

77

It's often easier to give up on something, or change your mind, in order to please other people. However, you should never compromise on what is truly important to you. It may be uncomfortable in the short-term to stick to your guns, but you will always be glad that you did.

Convinced By Consistency

Don't beat yourself up if you do something wrong - just keep trying until you get it right.

78

Everyone makes mistakes. It's how you view such mistakes that will determine how happy and successful you are. Instead of dwelling what when wrong, just look at what you can learn from it, and how you can do it differently in the future.

Convinced Over Time

Always set deadlines.

79

A goal is only really a dream without a deadline! We are hard-wired to be driven by time and deadlines, so set yourself some tough but achievable deadlines. Just doing this one simple thing will have a massive positive impact on your chances of success.

Convinced Over Time

Everybody has the same amount of time so make sure you make the most of yours.

80

Even billionaires only have twenty-four hours in a day just like you and I do. It's not what they do, but how they use their time that has allowed them to get to where they are. So always be asking yourself whether what you are currently doing is the absolute best use of your time.

Focus On People

Never forget to use the most important word in everyone's life.

81

Always try to use the other person's name as doing so will not only mark you out as someone different (as most people don't), but by default it will show that you have an interest in the other person. Studies have shown that people automatically take more notice when their name is used in a conversation.

Focus On People

Winning at all costs isn't always the only option.

82

When all is said and done, you only truly learn your lessons in life from the things that don't go the way you expect them to. Sure - aim to win as often as possible, but sometimes it's better to concede and learn something valuable, rather than winning just so that you can say you have done so.

Focus On Tools

Always make the most of the resources you have available to you.

83

Whether it is tools, technology, research, or other people - always take advantage of what you already have at your disposal. Don't try to reinvent the wheel, just begin by working with what you've already got and build from there - it's so much easier!

Focus On Tools

Don't use a lack of tools or resources as an excuse.

84

It's often the case that technology or tools don't work in the way that they should and therefore make your life more complicated as a result. If this happens just look at how you can carry on or how you can creatively come up with your own solution. By doing so you might just find a better way to use what you already have available.

Focus On Systems

Don't focus on the task at hand at the expense of the bigger picture.

85

It's easy to get sidetracked by more 'exciting' short-term tasks when a goal seems a long way off. So, make sure that you always check to see if what you are doing at the moment is actually contributing to your overall goals or not. If not - then either change what you're doing, or find yourself a more exciting goal!

Focus On Systems

Avoid taking one step forward and two steps back by being prepared properly.

86

There is a saying that 'luck is where preparation meets opportunity' and anyone who plans effectively will tell you that it is very true. Always map out a process or strategy for what you need to achieve as by doing so you will be able to easily have something to measure your progress against.

Focus On Information

Always prioritize which facts are the most important before making a start.

87

Taking action is always important, but it's also critical that you understand why you are doing so in the first place! There will always be facts or data that are more critical to the process than others, so make sure that you're aware of them before you start.

Focus On Information

Trust your judgment as you already DO know more than you think!

88

One of the biggest differences between those who are successful and those who wish they were is that successful people have the confidence to know they will discover what needs to be done, even if they don't currently have a clue! Start taking more risks and you'll be surprised at how you capable you really are.

Focus On Money

Do more than is expected of you and you will always be rewarded in the end.

89

Napoleon Hill called this 'going the extra mile' and listed it as one of the sixteen traits of some of the wealthiest people that ever lived. Start giving without expectation of a return, and you'll soon discover that you'll get so much more back than you can imagine!

Focus On Money

Be aware of the bottom line, whatever it may be.

90

Everyone is aware of the financial cost, but there is something as (if not more) important - the time cost involved in what you are doing. There are always ways to find more money, but you can never get back the time you have spent - so make sure that what you spend yours on is worthwhile.

Focus On Place

How you feel about what you do matters more than where you work or what your position is.

91

Some of the most content people on the planet do jobs that many people would hate! It doesn't matter what your industry is, what your job is, or what your business card says - if you're not happy doing what you do then no amount of money will change that fact.

Focus On Place

Sometimes the most rewarding times are those without a safety net.

92

It's the things that challenge you, which often scare you a little at the time, that become life-defining moments. There are always times you should play it safe, but every now and again allow yourself to make that leap as you never know what impact it can have on your life.

Focus On Time

Work within a deadline, but don't let it restrain you.

93

It is always important to set yourself deadlines as, if you don't, you are unlikely to achieve your targets. However, just because you have a deadline for a particular goal, don't let it restrict you if circumstances arise where you need to be a little more flexible. Life is never plain sailing and neither is the path to your goals!

Focus On Time

Keeping good time has a greater impact than you could imagine.

94

Who would you trust more - someone who always delivers on time, or someone who consistently comes up with excuses why they are running late? The impressions others have of you do count, whether you like it or not...so always make sure that you create good ones!

Focus On Activity

Never be busy just for the sake of it.

95

There is a huge difference between being busy and being productive. Being busy just for the sake of it is almost as bad as procrastinating if doing so doesn't contribute to getting you to where you need to go.

Focus On Activity

It's not about how much you do, but what you do, that will set you apart.

96

There are always tasks that have greater importance than others. Often these are the ones that require quick decisions on, or don't actually take very long to complete. Make sure that you focus your energy on the critical things - no matter how small they may be.

Bonus Tip

Allow yourself to take risks that challenge you.

97

You choose. You can either go through life trying to shield yourself from risk, yet ending up being exposed to it anyway at some point, or you can take control of your life and take calculated gambles based upon what you know. Life's too short not to take that step outside of your comfort zone occasionally.

Bonus Tip

Even the biggest projects always begin with a single step.

98

No matter what you are aiming for you won't get anywhere unless you take that first step. The hardest part of any project is the start, so just tackle what needs to be done and get going!

Bonus Tip

Be careful of 'analysis paralysis'.

99

Don't allow yourself to over-analyze when you should just be taking action. Sure, it helps to be well-informed and to have plans for future steps, but the best way to gather information is from feedback from what you have already done!

Bonus Tip

Some things are more important than 'success'.

100

If you pursue success at all costs then other areas of your life will undoubtedly suffer. Of course, be driven and focused on what you want to achieve, but never forget the importance of the truly important things in life like your health, family, and friends.

Bonus Tip

Don't force your opinions on others - let them make up their own.

101

Winning at the expense of other people may well seem to be a good thing in the short-term, but more often than not it's just a recipe for trouble! Instead, try to work in an atmosphere of empowerment where you allow other people to contribute their own ideas, and it will be a win-win for everyone.

Bonus Tip

Never allow yourself to be limited by what other people believe is possible.

102

Everyone's beliefs are shaped by their background and what has happened to them. Therefore, each person will look at every situation in their own unique way. With this in mind, don't be afraid to challenge the current thinking if you truly believe that you have found a 'better way' and can prove it!

Bonus Tip

Always give yourself time to think things through first.

103

Everything can be broken down into smaller pieces if you think it through well enough. Don't jump in feet first without giving some thought to the processes and steps involved. Being prepared in this way may take a little time at the start but such an investment will always pay off in the future.

Bonus Tip

You may not believe it, but you are 'World Class' at something!

104

Every single person has a talent or skill that other people wish they could have. You might not have an immediately obvious talent...but the more action you take towards your life goals, the greater chance you will have of discovering that truly 'World Class' talent that you DO have which is waiting inside you to be discovered!

Bonus Tip

Choose appreciation rather than envy.

105

It's easy to get jealous when you see others succeed or have a great lifestyle. By doing so, you are just focusing your energy on what you don't have, instead of looking at what action that person took in order to succeed. Instead, make an effort to appreciate what others have achieved and you will soon be on the way to joining them.

About JobEQ And The iWAM Questionnaire

jobEQ was created to help everyone find "the job of their lives". Our international network of partners helps people to find the right job which fits their attitude and motivation, as well as helping organizations to figure out what are the best motivational and attitudinal patterns for a job, thus creating a better match.

By comparing personal preferences with the ideal profile for a job (based on the patterns of the top performers), we help to get better results in recruiting, training & coaching. We also help managers to motivate people in better ways and help organizations to structure work in a way that motivates their staff more effectively.

Finally, we help organizations to study their organizational cultures, and take this into account when planning large change projects or mergers & acquisitions.

One of the key instruments for matching personal preferences and organizational needs is the iWAM questionnaire, which measures and analyzes in great depth the motivational and attitudinal patterns covered in this book.

If you want to learn more about your own strengths and weaknesses, try out the iWAM for free at: **www.jobEQ.net/SelfTest**

If you or your business are involved in any form of 'human resources management' then discover how jobEQ and the iWAM can help you at: **www.jobEQ.net/joinus**

About the Authors

Gary Vurnum

Gary Vurnum is one of the most popular self-improvement experts on the Internet. He is also the author of over twenty books on topics ranging from leadership and goal setting through to finding more spiritual meaning in your life.

Discover how Gary can help you truly achieve the life of your dreams at **www.Vurnum.com**

Patrick Merlevede

Patrick Merlevede's mission is to help people find the job of their lives. With this purpose in mind, he created jobEQ.com and a network of trainers, coaches, and consultants to work according this philosophy. He co-authored several books, including "7 Steps to Emotional Intelligence" and "Mastering Mentoring & Coaching with Emotional Intelligence".

If you want to reach Patrick, check out **www.merlevede.biz**

Notes

15365077R00063

Made in the USA
Lexington, KY
23 May 2012